The Beauty of
AUTUMN

through the artistry of
DAVID HULA

BEAUTIFUL AMERICA PUBLISHING COMPANY
9725 S.W. Commerce Circle
Wilsonville, Oregon 97070

Library of Congress Catalog Card Number 86-28668

ISBN: 0-89802-480-3

DESIGN & LAYOUT: Theodore E. Paul, Jr.
EDITOR: Beverly A. Paul
TYPESETTING: Oregon Typesetting
PRINTED: In Singapore through Creative Graphics International, Inc., N.Y., N.Y.
FIRST EDITION: December, 1986

To my mother and to the memory of my father.
Mom, I love you. Dad, I miss you.

PREFACE

Of all the magnificent sights with which nature has graced our planet, the autumn landscape is perhaps the grandest.

Tropical isles, deep canyons, rocky crags, and ocean expanses all are breathtaking and rightfully command our attention. Yet how can they surpass the sight of a dazzlingly colored forest—a forest which changed its wardrobe so abruptly, as if by magic? What other season or other natural phenomenon makes one feel so content, so glad to be alive, so grateful to be in its company? Autumn is the season of seasons—an unsurpassed natural spectacle which makes us cherish the gift of life by compelling us to recognize its beauty and the importance of taking steps to safeguard it. My realization of this fact has led to the production of this book.

Ever since childhood, autumn has been my favorite season. But it was not until I took my first trip to the north woods of Wisconsin and Michigan's Upper Peninsula that I recognized autumn for what it truly is.

It was only a one day journey, from Madison, Wisconsin to Lake Superior and back again, intended to be nothing more than a brief respite from the pressures of graduate study at the University of Wisconsin. Three other graduate students were my amiable companions. We stuffed ourselves into a tiny white jalopy of the type you might expect an impoverished graduate student to own, and rambled almost seven hundred miles in less than twenty-four hours, yet still found time for strolling along the beach of Lake Superior and hiking in to waterfalls on the Black River.

By the time we returned to Madison, my senses had been overwhelmed by the splendor of the north country autumn. The pictures I had taken that day had scarcely begun to capture the majesty of what I had witnessed; the multi-colored landscape, dotted with pristine lakes and laced with cozy brooks and thunderous rivers, seemed more like the Land of Oz than an earthly domain.

Gradually but inexorably, that one day sojourn developed into an eight year, ten thousand mile odyssey to photographically capture the majesty of autumn—a journey which led me back to the north woods at least six more times. But the north country is not the only part of our country which is at its best during autumn, so I have made a concerted effort to document this season over a wide range of regions. Many photographs are from the Great Lakes area (Wisconsin, Michigan, Minnesota), the Missouri Valley (Nebraska, Iowa, Missouri), the Kansas prairies, and the Colorado Rockies. Some photos are representative of the mixed forest zone covering New England, Southeast Canada, and the Upper Midwest, while others are representative of the open oak woodlands of the Midwest and portions of the Mid-Atlantic and the South; the Kansas prairie photography portrays the Great Plains, while the Colorado photographs are typical of the Rocky Mountain West. No photographic portfolio can be completely comprehensive, but the scenes in this collection do depict the essence of autumn as it appears in much of the United States and Canada.

One need not be purely an admirer of wilderness in order to consider autumn the most favored season. For it is during this time of year that farmers harvest their crops; that the more settled regions are at their picturesque best; that the sports fan had the greatest variety of activities to choose from as either spectator or participant. And it is not merely the few weeks of peak color which lend autumn its charm—the first hints of autumnal changes and the final stages of the fall transition may be less boisterous, but they are indeed poignant and more indicative of autumn's role in the cycle of seasons and of life. These photographs attempt to illustrate autumn in all its varying moods and forms. From the over four hundred suitable images I gathered during this photographic harvest, only the most significant and illuminating are included in this book.

A number of people thoughtfully assisted with this project. The landowners who allowed me to photograph on their property deserve my thanks; I'd particularly like to thank my good friend Jerry Sand, for permitting me to photograph in his woodland, which one autumn was so abundantly endowed with photogenic subjects that I fear I overlooked many. Several people gave me suggestions, both general and specific, about where I might find subjects to photograph. My good friend Jim Zaffiro was especially helpful in this regard; his knowledge of the north country was invaluable to this work, and when he served as a personal guide during some of my northward treks, his companionship was always a congenial pleasure. The staff at Beautiful America Publishing Company should be commended for their receptiveness to new ideas and commitment to high publishing standards. And of course, Mother Nature deserves the thanks of everyone for creating such a magnificent spectacle.

Capturing these images was a journey of love; an adventure in discovery, during which I was occasionally frightened, sometimes awestruck, but most frequently comforted by the sights I was privileged to behold. It is my fervant wish that you find as much enjoyment in viewing these images as I did in obtaining them.

David G. Hula

Autumn at its best.

Frosted leaves.

When the frost is on the punkin and the
    fodder's in the shock,
And you hear the kyouck and gobble of the
    struttin' turkey-cock,
And the clackin of the guineys, and the
    cluckin' of the hens,
And the rooster's hallylooyer as he tiptoes
    on the fence;
O, it's then the times a feller is a feelin'
    at his best,
With the risin' sun to greet him from a night
    of peaceful rest,
As he leaves the house, bareheaded, and
    goes out to feed the stock,
When the frost is on the punkin and the
    fodder's in the shock.

— from *When the Frost is on the Punkin*,
by James Whitcomb Riley (1849-1916).
Reprinted by permission of the Bobbs-
Merrill Company, publishers of the
Biographical Edition of *The Complete
Works of James Whitcomb Riley*,
copyright 1913.

AUTUMN

The transformation of deciduous tree leaves from the varying green shades of spring and summer into their brilliant autumnal hues is so captivating and so apparently mysterious that it might seem to be a work of magic performed purely for the delight of human onlookers. But nature's intention in staging this transition is more pragmatic than esthetic—the sole purpose being to prepare these trees for the onslaught of winter. And the process through which the leaves complete their life cycle is not beyond explanation.

The low humidity and gusty winds of winter result in slight moisture loss and wrinkling of the skin on the faces and hands of human beings. This problem is but a minor annoyance for us; for deciduous trees, however, the consequences of excess evaporation are much more severe. If they retained their green leaves during the winter months, more water would escape from their leaves than could be replaced through their roots in the dry frozen soil. So if a broad-leafed deciduous tree does not shed its leaves before winter strikes, its life will be imperiled. Before such trees could colonize the temperate regions, they had to develop a means of coping with this problem, and fortunately for us, they have done so successfully.

During the waning days of the summer, deciduous trees receive a signal that the time to shed their leaves has arrived. What is this signal? Although we can't be totally certain, it appears that the shortening amount of daylight, rather than the lowering of atmospheric temperature, is the catalyst for this process. Exactly when a tree responds to this signal—whatever it may be—depends upon a number of factors, including the tree species and the altitude and latitude of the tree. Although different trees may respond to this signal at different times or may even have different signals, the manner in which they respond is basically the same for all.

At the base of each leaf stalk, a zone of cells called the abscission layer is formed once the signal is received. This layer dries out and loosens itself from the surrounding cells. Then a layer of cork cells forms below the abscission layer, which will cover the spot where the leaf breaks off. The formation of the abscission and cork layers causes the vascular bundles at the base of the leaf stalk to become clogged. The leaf is now no longer able to receive the nutrients it needs to manufacture chlorophyll. Well-nourished leaves contain a number of pigments, including not only chlorophyll but also xanthophyll, carotene, and anthocyanins. All these pigments decompose once their source of nourishment is cut off, but the chlorophyll fades before the other pigments. During the summer months, the green of the chlorophyll predominates over the other pigments, But as the chlorophyll fades, the other pigments—which were present all along—now have the chance to show their true colors: carotene and xanthophyll being yellow-gold, the anthocyanins reddish, and the tannins of certain oaks, brown. The fall color displays are now present for all to see.

But the transformation is not quite complete. The abscission layer eventually breaks, so that only the vascular bundles hold the leaf to the branch. It is only a matter of time before the brisk autumn winds sever this last obstacle to the leaf's downward flight. When the leaf finally descends to the forest floor, it develops into humus, enriching the soil and further contributing to the preservation of life.

Even the most casual observer will notice that the coniferous evergreens do not shed their leaves on such a sudden and monumental scale. But they too must cope with the problem of excessive evaporation during the winter. Their needle-like, waxy leaves reduce the amount of water they lose, as compared to the broad-leafed species, but they too lose their leaves, although at a much slower rate.

The changing of color and subsequent shedding of leaves is a survival adaptation that is evident to everyone. But in order to continue the life cycle, the trees must eventually replace the lost leaves, since leaves serve as vital food manufacturers for the tree and for all life as they convert water, light, and carbon dioxide into carbohydrates, with the aid of chlorophyll. The process of developing new leaves is much less visible but no less essential to the tree's welfare. And during autumn, this task is also perpetuated.

Beginning in midsummer, the trees devote some of their food and energy to the formation of new buds, which in turn will become new leaves in the forthcoming spring. These buds—called winter buds—are covered with a protective layer of scales. They are visible during the winter, if you look closely, along with the scars of previously shed leaves. Although these buds are difficult, if not impossible to detect during the autumn months, the process of creating them is nevertheless underway during that time.

Trees are not the only plants which must somehow deal with the rigors of winter and insure the survival of the species; smaller plants also face this dilemma. The biennials and perennials are able to withstand at least one winter without perishing, but the annuals are not so fortunate—they dedicate their short existences to the production of seeds. Once these seeds are produced and distributed through a variety of ingenious means, they soon expire, exhausted by their efforts. But despite the many hazards these seeds face from hungry birds and infertile ground, enough of them germinate and flourish to perpetuate the species.

The plant kingdom is not unique in having to make preparations for winter. All animals in temperate regions must also deal with the inclement weather lurking just over the climatic horizon, and many of their autumnal activities are directed to this end.

During early autumn, large ungulates such as deer, elk, and moose are more concerned with mating matters than with winter preparations. The adult males vocally advertise their eligibility and battle each other for the privilege of siring the next generation. Only then do they see fit to cope with the coming of winter. More diminutive creatures such as sparrows, chickadees, and woodpeckers are adapted to life in a cold and snowy realm. For them, autumn is a time for "business as usual." There are no youngsters to raise, no migrations to undertake. Fall is their season to eat, drink, and be merry until the more austere environment of winter presents itself. But many creatures, regardless of size, are not capable of finding life-sustaining food and warmth during winter without taking preparatory measures. And so it is that the bears and woodchucks gorge themselves on autumn's bounty to store up fat reserves for their long winter's sleep, and that the beavers and squirrels accumulate inventories of food to be tapped as the need arises.

Put yourself for a moment in the position of a turkey or a bat or any other creature which must deal with winter. There are several alternative strategies you may use to face this challenge. You can hibernate the winter weeks away like a black bear, after putting on enough fat to qualify for sumo wrestler status. You can horde food and then eat it as necessary. Or, like the mink, you can evolve a warm coat of fur and sharp teeth that enable you to capture live prey, and carry on the winter in basically the same way you do the rest of the year. You may even adopt the "orangutan strategy"— simply live on certain Southeast Asian islands and avoid colder regions entirely. But the most visible strategy to our eyes is that of the snow goose— live in the north country during the summer, then migrate to warmer climes before winter's fury strikes. Migration is the preferred survival strategy for avoiding winter heat loss and starvation, for not only the snow goose, but also for most kinds of waterfowl and indeed, most kinds of birds. Mammals may employ the migration strategy on a minor scale—for example, elk may descend from the high country to lower elevations during the wintertime—but it is the birds who are the most notable migrants, both in terms of numbers and length of journeys.

Many avian migrants prefer to remain out of sight as they head for their winter homes in Brazil or Peru. The warblers are shy and furtive at all times, and in the fall, while migrating, they are likely to remain true to character. Like miniature feathered spies on undercover missions, their plumage changes from its brilliant coloration of spring and summer to a mottled version of its former self, making it difficult to observe them, or, if seen, to identify them. They sulk in the bushes and undergrowth by day, and fly by night. Yet, after going to all this trouble to be secretive, they may allow one to approach them quite closely, apparently ignoring the observer, as long as no sudden moves are made. Once you have discovered their whereabouts, they don't seem to mind, as long as you don't interfere with their mission.

The waterfowl are equally determined to reach their destinations, and are far easier to spot than the warblers and other songbirds as they undertake their autumnal journeys. To use the word "visible" to describe them is to understate their presence, for they form into flocks numbering in the tens of thousands, all of them honking in an unorchestrated chorus, so that they can be both seen and heard from miles away. The sight and sound of such an exodus can be every bit as soul-stirring as the witnessing of the most riotous, broad-sweeping fall color display. But the waterfowl do not migrate in order to entertain us. As with the advent of the forest clad in red, yellow, and orange, the pleasure we obtain in viewing them is but an incidental side effect tangential to nature's purpose.

Scientists often chide the public for anthropomorphizing—attributing human characteristics to animals. But it is equally incorrect to think that humans have nothing in common with other creatures. For after all, humans are also animals, though special ones. Like all forms of life, whether animal or plant, we face the question of how to utilize the autumn months to prepare for the upcoming winter. And our responses to this challenge do not always differ that much from theirs.

Food gathering is a fall activity humans share with the beasts. Whether shooting a pheasant, plucking a pumpkin out of a pumpkin patch, collecting Halloween candy, picking edible wild mushrooms, gleaning cranberries from a bog, or removing corn from a field with the aid of a thirty thousand dollar combine, the human harvester is engaged in a pursuit not all that different from the beaver building up its storehouse of aspen and poplar branches under the water near its lodge. The retired couple who, once November arrives, pack their bags and head from their summer house in Vermont to their winter retreat in Florida are exhibiting behavior not altogether dissimilar from that of the whooping crane, which finds its nesting grounds in Alberta to be just a bit too cold for year-round occupancy. But not all human activity in the autumn has an animal counterpart.

Since man is the only creature which purposely uses fire, the chopping of firewood and accumulation of a quaint-looking woodpile for use as fuel rather than food has not been observed in the animal kingdom. The development of technology not only enables us to take advantage of fire, but also to devote some of our precious autumn time to pursuits not directly related to survival, such as playing football. Or watching football. Or playing baseball. Or watching baseball. Or playing basketball. Or watching basketball. Or playing hockey. Or watching hockey. Who would deny that autumn is the premier season for sports participants and sports aficionados alike?

Despite what ardent baseball fans may say, football is the most popular sport in the United States. Autumn weekends offer a multitude of games to choose from, ranging from top-level NFL action in ninety thousand seat stadiums in giant metropolises to impromptu grade-school games in the backyards of isolated villages. Barring the injuries, deaths, gambling losses, and controversial outcomes accompanying the sport, its impact on the national welfare is positive; it may serve as an outlet for the warlike tendencies of the populace which might otherwise be vented in less acceptable ways. But autumn offers another activity far less violent, far more precious, and much more uplifting to the soul: taking a walk through the woods or a drive through the countryside to observe nature's colorful handiwork. Football can be played anytime, and watched at least until mid-January, while the peak fall foliage will vanish in a shorter time than it took to make its appearance. So try to make room for both football watching and leaf-looking. They are both worthwhile pursuits.

As with all natural phenomena, autumn retains elements of mystery. We do not know all the details of what triggers the process of leaf color change, or of how migrating birds decide when to begin their autumnal journeys, and how they guide themselves to their destinations. We can't even explain why the sport of football is so popular in the United States but so ill-received in other parts of the world.

Yet autumn is not a total mystery. The basic process by which leaves change color is well established. The reasons for migration are clear, even if the details of this behavior are not. We also know, of course, that autumn evolves because the tilt of the earth's axis changes as it revolves around the sun—when the north pole begins to tilt away from the sun, autumn begins in the northern hemisphere and spring commences in the southern hemisphere. Later, when the tilt of the earth's axis reverses itself, the seasons respond accordingly.

Perhaps the most significant fact of all about this season is that the United States and Canada offer the world's finest displays of fall color. True, the Soviet Union, China, and Europe, among other places, exhibit autumnal colors in the foliage of their forests. Most would agree, however, that the United States and Canada feature the most spectacular autumnal vistas—the earth's most noteworthy manifestations of nature's most beautiful season. Proper use will emphasize and guarantee the fact that our autumn forests are truly national treasures, eminently worthy of both observation and preservation. Enjoy. . . Enjoy!

22 — Architectural enhancement.

23 — Regal splendor.

Soft muted beauty.

26 — Flaming fall fashion.
27 — Transparent artistry.

28 — Pre-game warm-up.

29 — Last of the ninth.

30 — Golden tree house.

31 — I am already on this line!

31

Nature's centerpiece.

34 — The perfect setting.

35 — On the way to church.

36 — The last of the season.
37 — Goblin greeters.

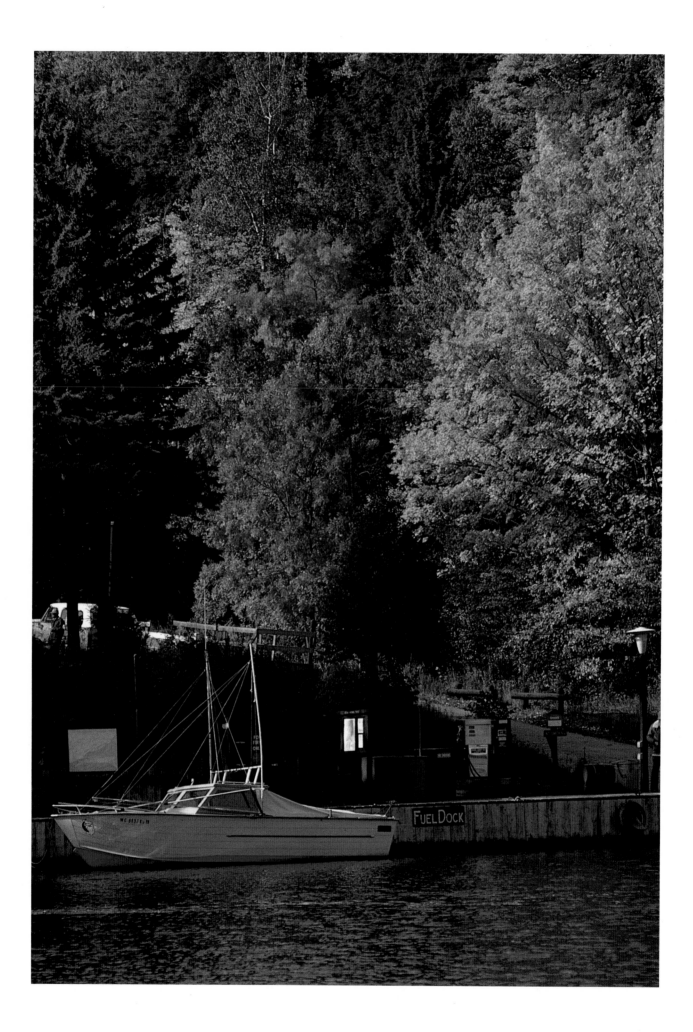

38 — Autumn pleasure craft.
39 — Spectacular color.

39

Autumn's patchwork quilt.

42 — Feeding time.

43 — Up close and beautiful.

44 — Nature's color combination.
45 — Woodland splendor.

46 — The old covered bridge.

47 — Inside looking out.

47

48 — Rushing water, autumn's music.

49 — Serenity.

50 — The nature trail.

51 — Movin' on.

52 — Fall is for planting.

53 — Great results.

54 — Steady as she goes.

55 — Who is the home team?

55

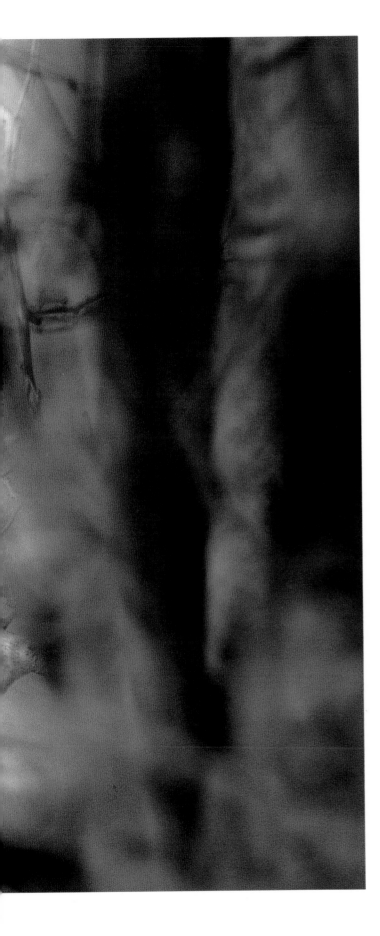

Sepia spectacular.

60 — No need for decorations.

61 — The cannon's flash.

62 — Overhead brilliance.

63 — Solid gold.

64 — Drive careful.
65 — Dangerous intersection.

66 — Autumn's Goldenrod.

67 — A matched pair.

67

68 — Rustic beauty.

69 — Cliffside of color.

70 — The Master's touch.

71 — Walls of color.

Our golden halo.

74 — Airborne thistle seed.

75 — The thistle seed gourmet.

76 — Of fall's past.
77 — Prior education.

78 — Fields of beauty.

79 — Flaming contrast.

80 — Natural enhancement.

81 — Winter's wonder.

82 — The splendor of the Rockies.

83 — Lofty visitors.

84 — Christmas colors.
85 — Frosty decorations.

85

86 — Holy timber.

87 — Red-headed drill instructor.

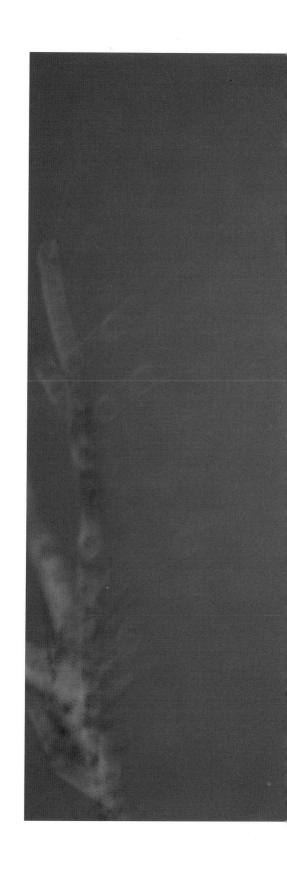

Mountain majesty.

90 — 91   The classic green and gold mountain
mantle.

92 — Prairie skies.
93 — Single sentinel.

93

94 — Prairie ponies.

95 — Pastoral grazing.

96 — The scarlet accent.

97 — Beautiful close-up.

98 — Stocking up for winter.

99 — Just about ready.

99

102 — Bygone autumns.

103 — Rustic beauty.

Autumn, the prelude to winter.

107

108 — Fence-line magic.

109 — Autumnal vista.

109

110 — Give Thanks.
111 — For what?

112 — The big game.
113 — The little one.

114 — A beaver's home.
115 — The fruits of his labor.

116 — Typical autumn setting.

117 — Impossible to resist.

118 — Autumn walks.
119 — Hand in hand.

119

120 — The subtle tones on shore.

121 — Just as artistic in the water.

122 — The fall harvest.
123 — Harvest playground.

124 — Airforce alert.

125 — The ground troops.

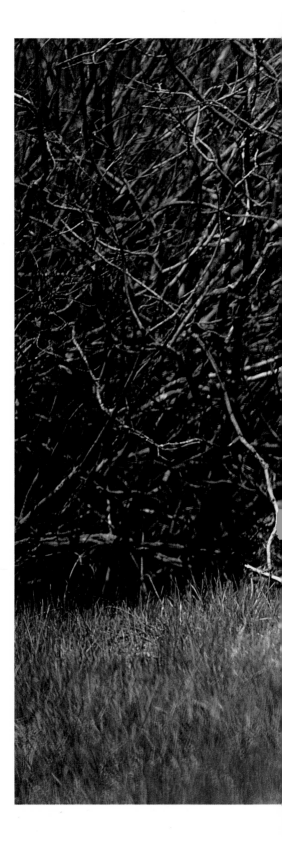

126 — Breath-taking foliage.

127 — Up-close artistry.

127

128 — Turkey Trot Lane.
129 — You guessed it!

129

130 — Nature's icing.

131 — Crystal decoration.

132 — Intense interest.

133 — The winged reason.

134 — The rustic fall scene.

135 — The wise visitor.

135

The autumn colors that stir men's souls.

138 — Cattail collection.

139 — A visitor in the hollyhocks.

140 — Harvest moon.

141 — Autumn serenade.

141